Lighten Your Hair

and Solve Household Problems

Betsy Rossen Elliot

Contents

Beauty and Grooming • 2

Home Remedies • 8

Cleaning • 14

Cooking and Laundry • 20

House and Home • 26

Beauty and Grooming

Look and feel your best with the help of the citrus team! Consider the capabilities of lemons, limes, and oranges to enhance your coiffure, relax your body and soul, and bump up your grooming regimen. Other residents of the pantry and produce drawer can give you the spa treatment as well. What's more, you're saving money and trips to the store. Talk about refreshing and restorative!

BEAUTY BASICS

Hair Care

◆ Blond highlights will magically appear if you rinse your hair with a mixture of ¼ cup ReaLemon Lemon Juice and ¾ cup water. For extra lightening, sit in the sun until your hair dries.

◆ Swimming in a chlorinated pool can give dyed blond hair a greenish tint. One treatment for removing the green is Campbell's Tomato Juice. Rub enough into your hair to cover it, leave on 2 minutes, then rinse.

◆ Make yourself a simple, inexpensive hairspray. In a saucepan, boil 2 cups water. Add 2 lemons, peeled and finely chopped. Simmer over low heat until lemons are soft. After the mixture cools, pour it through a strainer and then into a labeled spray bottle. Add 1 tablespoon of 100-proof vodka; shake well. Dilute with a little water if the spray is too sticky.

- Attack dandruff with lemon juice. Rub 1 tablespoon ReaLemon Lemon Juice into dry hair, down to the scalp. Shampoo and rinse as usual. Then, rinse hair again using a solution of 2 cups water and 2 tablespoons lemon juice. Repeat every other day for 1 week.

Hand-y Hints

- Soak your fingernails in ReaLemon Lemon Juice for 10 minutes, then rinse well with warm water. This will help strengthen and brighten fingernails.

- If your hands smell like garlic, rub a cut lemon over them.

- After working with fruit that stains, rinse your hands with ReaLemon Lemon Juice to get rid of the color.

Pamper and Primp

- Reenergize your tired feet by massaging ReaLime Lime Juice into the skin.

- Fight cellulite with an herbal wrap that's a fraction of the price fancy spas charge. Combine ½ cup grapefruit juice, 1 cup Crisco Pure Corn Oil, and 2 teaspoons McCormick Ground Thyme. Massage mixture into trouble spots such as hips, thighs, and buttocks. Cover areas with GLAD Cling Wrap; hold a heating pad over each section for 5 minutes.

Cool Bath for a Hot Day

½ cup ReaLemon Lemon Juice

½ cup ReaLime Lime Juice

6 drops McCormick Pure Lemon Extract

½ cup ARM & HAMMER Baking Soda (if your home has hard water)

Mix ingredients in a bowl; pour into tepid bathwater. Enjoy a soothing soak!

- Give a fresh fragrance to your bath by floating lemon peels on the surface.

- Make yourself a soothing milk bath by adding ½ cup Carnation Instant Nonfat Dry Milk to warm bathwater. Milk soothes the skin.

FACIALS AND CLEANSERS

- Try this facial to tone and soften your skin. Beat 1 large egg white; stir in the juice of half a lemon (about 1½ tablespoons ReaLemon Lemon Juice). Apply to face and neck. After 20 minutes, rinse, pat dry, then apply some witch hazel with a Rite Aid cotton ball.

- Cool and nourish your face with a mask made from the juice of ¼ orange (about 2 tablespoons Tropicana Pure Premium orange juice) and 1 teaspoon plain Dannon yogurt. Mix well; smooth on with your fingertips. After 5 minutes, rinse with cool water.

- Give yourself a fresh-fruit facial. Puree the following in a blender or food processor: 1 ounce Tropicana Pure Premium orange juice, 6 strawberries, ½ apple, and ½ pear. Spread a thin layer of Sue Bee Honey on your face, followed by the fruit blend. Wait at least 30 minutes; rinse with warm water, then gently pat dry.

- For a refreshing facial, mix 1 tablespoon Carnation Instant Nonfat Dry Milk; ½ peeled cucumber, minced; and 1 teaspoon plain Dannon yogurt. Apply to face, let dry, and rinse.

- Whip up a cleanser that's right for all skin types. In a blender or food processor, combine 1 cup dried orange peel, 1 cup shelled almonds, and 1 cup Old Fashioned Quaker Oats. Chop into a fine powder. Place a small amount in your palm, add a few drops of water, and rub onto your face, being careful to avoid the eyes. Rinse with warm water; pat dry. Keep the powder at room temperature, stored in an airtight container.

- Apples have a combination of tough-and-tender chemicals that is perfect for facial treatments. Try this cleanser: Make a paste of 2 teaspoons Mott's apple juice, 2 teaspoons red wine, and 1 tablespoon ground Old Fashioned Quaker Oats. Add more juice or wine if necessary. Apply mixture to face and throat; let dry for 20 to 30 minutes. Gently rinse off with warm water.

- Tone and clarify your skin with an apple astringent. Pour these ingredients into a bottle: ½ cup Mott's apple juice, 4 tablespoons 100-proof vodka, 1 tablespoon Sue Bee Honey, and 1 teaspoon Morton Sea Salt. Cap bottle; shake well. Twice a day, apply astringent to your face and neck using a Rite Aid cotton ball.

- Dry milk can be used as a makeup remover. Mix 1 teaspoon Carnation Instant Nonfat Dry Milk with warm water and apply to your face using a Rite Aid cotton ball. Rinse clean.

THE SKINNY ON SKIN

Blemishes

- Apply ReaLemon Lemon Juice to blackheads using a Rite Aid cotton ball or a Q-tips cotton swab. Leave the juice on overnight. In the morning, rinse your face with cool water. Repeat every night for 1 week.

- To dry up pimples quickly, apply ReaLemon Lemon Juice several times a day using a Q-tips cotton swab.

- Fight blackheads and pimples by washing your face with the juice of a fresh lime (or 3 tablespoons ReaLime Lime Juice) in a glass of boiled whole milk. Add 1 teaspoon glycerin if your skin is dry.

Spot Check

- Bothered by freckles or age spots? Dissolve a pinch of Domino Sugar in 2 tablespoons ReaLemon Lemon Juice. Apply the mixture to each spot with a Rite Aid cotton ball or a Kleenex facial tissue. Repeat every few days until the spots have lightened to your liking.

- Another trick to lighten the effects of age and the sun: Mix 3 tablespoons ReaLime Lime Juice, 3 tablespoons ReaLemon Lemon Juice, 4 tablespoons plain Dannon yogurt, and 2 tablespoons Sue Bee Honey. Once or twice a week, gently rub the mixture into each spot with your fingertips. Store in a covered container in your refrigerator.

Smooth News

- To soften calluses and other rough spots on your feet, heels, and elbows, rub the affected areas with half a lemon.

- Remove flaky skin by dipping a Rite Aid cotton ball in milk and applying it to the area. Rinse with cool water.

MORE GROOMING TIPS
Brushing and Breath

- Here's a surprising makeshift toothbrush: Take a piece of lemon or lime peel and rub the inside of it over your teeth and gums. Both contain chemicals that fight gum disease and help whiten teeth.

- Another way to keep your mouth clean and healthy is to rub your teeth and gums several times a day with a paste made of ReaLime Lime Juice and Morton Salt.

- Freshen your breath with lime juice. Mix the juice of 1 lime (or 3 tablespoons ReaLime Lime Juice) and 1 teaspoon Sue Bee Honey in a glass of water. Drink between meals and at bedtime.

- Take care of garlic breath by taking a bite out of an apple. Then brush your teeth.

At Your Best

- On a diet? Try this to curb your appetite. Mix 2 tablespoons grapefruit juice with 1 tablespoon Hain Safflower Oil; take before each meal.

- This handy tonic works as a deodorant, tightens pores, and eases sunburn and other minor burns. In a clean glass jar (with lid), combine the juice of 1 lemon (about 3 tablespoons ReaLemon Lemon Juice), 1 cup witch hazel, and 3 tablespoons coarsely chopped cucumber. Close up with lid and let stand for 2 days; strain out cucumber. Store remaining liquid in a capped bottle in your refrigerator. Apply with a Rite Aid cotton ball.

Home Remedies

When you were a child, did lemon juice and honey combine to quiet your nighttime cough?

Now, the healing qualities of fruits, veggies, and other cooking products are ready to help all the members of your family. A lime can relieve a headache. Lemon juice relieves the itch of poison ivy. Orange juice will help banish nausea.

Of course, these simple remedies are no substitute for professional medical care. Do not hesitate to contact your doctor or go to an emergency room if your condition warrants it.

RELIEF IS HERE

Aches and Pains

- Ease that throbbing headache. Cut a lime in half and rub it on your forehead.

- Make your own ice pack. Freeze unpopped Orville Redenbacher's popcorn in a pint- or quart-size GLAD Food Storage Zipper Bag; apply to bumps and bruises. Refreeze as necessary.

- Soak a thick slice of onion in Heinz Distilled White Vinegar, then apply onion slice to a bruise. Folk tradition claims this will advance the healing process.

- If you have a boil, make a compress with Contadina Tomato Paste and cover the boil. The acids in the paste will bring the boil to a head and relieve the pain.

My Mouth Hurts!

◆ Dab a little ReaLemon Lemon Juice on that irritating cold sore or fever blister. It acts as an astringent and promotes healing.

◆ Cold milk helps speed the healing of a cold sore. Apply a milk-soaked Rite Aid cotton ball to the sore to ease the pain.

◆ Canker sores are annoying and painful. Put 2 teaspoons McCormick Rubbed Sage in a cup of hot water; let steep for about 10 minutes. Add ½ teaspoon ReaLemon Lemon Juice. Gargle with the warm solution.

◆ When your mouth is on fire from spicy food, water only makes it worse. Instead, drink milk. It dilutes the oils that cause the spiciness.

Bites, Stings, Itches & Burns

◆ Treat insect bites or poison ivy with a mixture of 1 quart milk, 2 tablespoons Morton Salt, and ice. Apply with a cloth to affected skin 3 times a day for 20 minutes at a time.

◆ Soothe the sting of a bee or fire ant with a drop of ReaLime Lime Juice. Note: If you show any signs of an allergic reaction to the sting or bite, seek immediate medical attention.

◆ Use ReaLemon Lemon Juice to relieve the itching and alleviate a rash from poison ivy. Apply directly to affected areas.

- Use citric power to stop the itch of poisonous plants, insect bites, or allergic reactions. Make a paste of ReaLemon Lemon Juice and Argo Corn Starch; rub gently on the itchy spots.

- Calm those itchy hives with milk. Soak a cloth in a bowl of cold milk and apply to affected areas for 10 minutes. Wring out, soak in milk again, and reapply.

- Whole milk can ease sunburn pain. Soak a cloth and apply to skin; let sit for 20 minutes, then rinse skin with lukewarm water.

Insomnia

- The sleep-inducing properties of warm milk are legendary. Zap a microwavable mug of milk on high for 1 minute; stir and test temperature before drinking. Or, heat the milk in a small saucepan over low heat until it's warm, but not boiling.

- Here's a more "heavy-duty" recipe to help you sleep. Stir the following into 1 cup of warm milk: 1 tablespoon Carnation Instant

I Guess It Sounds Better than "Orangeys" or "Lemoneys"

Scurvy is one of the oldest-recognized nutritional deficiencies. The problem is a lack of vitamin C (ascorbic acid), leading to gum disease, painful and stiff joints, inhibited healing of wounds, and anemia. From the late 1400s on, scurvy became the number one cause of disability and death among sailors. Dr. James Lind, a Scottish naval surgeon, proved in 1753 that scurvy could be prevented and even cured by drinking orange or lemon juice. Citrus juice soon was so common aboard British ships that the sailors were nicknamed "limeys."

Nonfat Dry Milk, 2 tablespoons Sue Bee Honey, and 1 tablespoon brewer's yeast. Drink before going to bed.

Tummy Troubles

◆ Try this elixir as a remedy for nausea: Mix 1 cup water, 10 drops ReaLime Lime Juice, and ½ teaspoon Domino Sugar. Stir in ¼ teaspoon ARM & HAMMER Baking Soda. Sip it slowly.

◆ Relieve nausea by mixing ½ cup Tropicana Pure Premium orange juice, 2 tablespoons Karo Light Corn Syrup, a pinch of Morton Salt, and ½ cup water in a lidded jar or container. Refrigerate. Take 1 tablespoon every 30 minutes until the queasiness quits.

◆ Bland foods ease nausea, hence the wisdom of this folk remedy: Cover a bowl of unbuttered, unsalted Orville Redenbacher's popcorn (popped without oil) with boiling water. Eat the resulting mush slowly.

Colds, Coughs & Sore Throats

◆ Sip this warm elixir to reduce a fever. Combine 1½ teaspoons McCormick Cream of Tartar, ½ teaspoon ReaLemon Lemon Juice, 2½ cups warm water, and ½ teaspoon Sue Bee Honey. Drink slowly.

◆ Make your own cough syrup by mixing 4 tablespoons ReaLemon Lemon Juice, 1 cup Sue Bee Honey, and ½ cup Colavita Extra Virgin Olive Oil. Heat, stirring vigorously. Take 1 teaspoon every 2 hours.

◆ Try this nighttime cough suppressant. Bring 2 cups of water to a boil. Stir in 2 sliced lemons, ½ teaspoon

McCormick Ground Ginger, 2 tablespoons Sue Bee Honey, and 2 tablespoons Domino Sugar. Bring to a boil again; reduce heat and simmer until mixture becomes a thick syrup. If you wish, add 1 ounce liqueur or brandy. Take 1 to 2 teaspoons after mixture cools.

◆ Honey promotes the flow of mucus and is great for coughs. Mix 1 tablespoon Sue Bee Honey with 1 cup hot water and 2 drops ReaLemon Lemon Juice. Sip for relief.

◆ Drink a warm cup of Lipton tea mixed with ReaLemon Lemon Juice and Sue Bee Honey to soothe a sore throat or laryngitis.

◆ Lessen the pain of a sore throat with this drink. Mix 3 tablespoons ReaLime Lime Juice, 1 tablespoon Dole Pineapple Juice, and 1 teaspoon Sue Bee Honey in a glass of water.

◆ Make a healing potion for bronchitis. Slice an onion into a bowl, cover with Sue Bee Honey, and let stand overnight. Take 1 teaspoon of the liquid 4 times a day.

WHAT ELSE AILS YOU?

◆ When the hiccups just won't go away, cut off a small slice of lemon (without the peel). Place it under your tongue and suck once; hold the juice for 10 seconds, then swallow the juice. Many folks swear by this!

◆ If you're trying to quit smoking or drinking, lessen cravings by sucking on a slice of lime. This will also replace some of the vitamins, calcium, and phosphates your system may have lost.

- Drink a cup of hot Lipton tea with 1 or 2 teaspoons of ReaLime Lime Juice for fast relief from diarrhea.

- Not fond of hot tea? Here's an alternative diarrhea remedy. In a blender or food processor, puree 1 peeled and cored apple; add 1 teaspoon ReaLime Lime Juice, a few drops of Sue Bee Honey, and a pinch of McCormick Ground Cinnamon. Drink the whole concoction. Call your doctor if the diarrhea lasts more than a day.

- Another remedy for diarrhea: Stir 1 teaspoon carob powder into ¼ cup Mott's Classic apple sauce. Eat 2 or 3 times during the day, but slowly.

- Get relief from constipation with a mix of ½ cup Mott's Classic apple sauce, 4 to 6 chopped prunes, and 1 tablespoon bran. Eat just before bedtime—things should feel better in the morning.

- Constipated? Try this drink before breakfast: Mix 1 cup warm water, 4 tablespoons ReaLemon Lemon Juice, and Sue Bee Honey to taste.

- Flush out pepper or other eye irritants with a few drops of milk.

- Make your own elixir to heal or prevent a urinary tract infection. Boil 8 ounces Ocean Spray cranberry juice; reduce heat and add 2 teaspoons powdered echinacea root. Simmer for 15 minutes. Remove from heat, then add 1 teaspoon powdered goldenseal root. Steep for 20 minutes. Strain and add about 1 teaspoon ReaLemon Lemon Juice. Drink warm or iced.

Cleaning

The fresh scent and astringency of lemon have long given it a place of pride in the cleaning cabinet. You'll find that the extent of its power—alone and with other common household products—matches its reputation.

Odors? Soap scum? Grease? Tarnish? Plain ol' dirt? Their days are numbered when whole fruits, peels, and juice are in your arsenal.

ALL-AROUND CLEANING

The Walls Have Smears

◆ Here's a recipe for a homemade cleaner that's great for getting dirty fingerprints off walls and door frames (among other things). In a clean spray bottle, mix together 1 teaspoon ARM & HAMMER Baking Soda, 1 teaspoon 20 Mule Team Borax, 2 teaspoons ReaLemon Lemon Juice, 3 teaspoons Dawn dishwashing liquid, and 2 cups hot water. Make sure you clearly label the bottle; shake well before each use.

Furniture and Floors

◆ Try this recipe for furniture polish: In a glass jar with a tight-fitting lid, mix ¼ cup ReaLemon Lemon Juice or fresh lemon juice with ½ cup Crisco Pure Vegetable Oil. Apply to wood furniture with a cotton cloth, rubbing in a small

amount at a time. Kept out of direct sunlight, this mixture can be stored for several months.

Homemade Glass Cleaner

3 tablespoons ReaLemon Lemon Juice
½ cup Rite Aid isopropyl rubbing alcohol
¼ teaspoon Dawn dishwashing liquid

Add all ingredients to a spray bottle, fill the bottle the rest of the way with water, and shake well to mix. Use as you would any commercial window cleaner. Be sure to clearly label the bottle before storing.

◆ To remove scratches from a wooden table, increase the amount of lemon juice in the previous furniture polish recipe so that you're using equal parts ReaLemon Lemon Juice and Crisco Pure Vegetable Oil. With a soft, clean cotton cloth, gently rub the mixture into the wood, buffing out the scratches. Repeat as needed until scratches are gone.

◆ Here's an alternative lemon-based furniture polish. Mix the following in a bowl: 2 tablespoons ReaLemon Lemon Juice, 10 drops lemon oil, and 4 drops Colavita Extra Virgin Olive Oil. Using a circular motion, gently apply to furniture with a soft, clean cotton cloth.

◆ A glass tabletop will shine brightly if you rub it gently with a few drops of ReaLemon Lemon Juice. Dry with a Scott Towel, then polish with a crumpled-up piece of newspaper.

◆ Keep leather upholstery looking its best: Every 3 months, use a clean cloth to wipe on a small quantity of skim milk.

Citrus at the Cinema

One of the most famous scenes involving a citrus fruit appears in the 1931 film classic *The Public Enemy.* At the breakfast table, gangster Tom Powers (James Cagney) suddenly smashes half a grapefruit into the face of Kitty (Mae Clarke). The shot was an unscripted practical joke on the crew, concocted by Cagney and Clarke. They never dreamed it would be used in the final version, but director William Wellman decided otherwise. A clip of just that grapefruit interaction can look to casual viewers like comic relief; in context, the moment is quite ominous. Women's groups nationwide protested the on-screen abuse of actress Clarke.

◆ To remove ink stains from carpets or rugs, apply a paste made of milk and Argo Corn Starch. Let dry a few hours, then brush or vacuum off.

Precious Metals and More

◆ Make your silver sparkle! In a bowl, mix 1 tablespoon ReaLemon Lemon Juice (or 1 tablespoon Heinz Distilled White  Vinegar), ½ cup Carnation Instant Nonfat Dry Milk, and 1½ cups water. Place your silver in the bowl; let sit overnight. Rinse and dry thoroughly. Double or even triple this recipe if necessary to accommodate your silver.

◆ If you need clean silver now instead of tomorrow morning, pour ReaLemon Lemon Juice over the pieces you want to clean. Polish with a soft, clean cotton cloth.

- Clean slightly tarnished brass or copper with half a lemon or lime dipped in Morton Salt.

- Use either of these homemade pastes to clean brass or copper. For the first, mix enough ReaLemon Lemon Juice and either ARM & HAMMER Baking Soda or McCormick Cream of Tartar to form a paste. The second combines ReaLemon Lemon Juice, Morton Salt, and Quaker Yellow Corn Meal. Whichever paste you make, rub it onto brass or copper using a soft, dry cloth; rinse with cool water and dry.

- Bring back the shine on piano keys and gilt picture frames by rubbing carefully with a cloth dipped in milk.

ASSIGNMENT: THE KITCHEN

Sinks

- Combine ReaLemon Lemon Juice and Morton Salt until mixture reaches the consistency of toothpaste. Apply this to brass, copper, or stainless-steel sinks and fixtures. Scrub gently, then rinse with water.

- Loosen mineral deposits on faucets by sponging on ReaLemon Lemon Juice, letting it soak in for a while, then scrubbing off.

- To remove odors from a garbage disposal, cut up a lemon, toss it in, and grind it up. Orange and lemon peels also work.

Appliances

◆ Remove dried-on food or detergent from the chrome inside your dishwasher by rubbing it with a piece of lemon. Rinse by wiping with a damp cloth, then rub dry with a clean, dry cloth.

◆ Deodorize and clean out hard-water stains from the inside of your dishwasher by running it using powdered Country Time Lemonade mix instead of detergent. The ascorbic acid in the powder helps the cleaning action.

◆ Spills on stovetops and in ovens are no match for this mixture: Make a paste of ReaLemon Lemon Juice, water, and ARM & HAMMER Baking Soda. Apply to spills, let sit 15 minutes, and then scrub and rinse with water and an O-Cel-O sponge.

Windows

◆ Wash greasy kitchen windows with a solution of 2 tablespoons ReaLemon Lemon Juice, ½ cup Heinz Distilled White Vinegar, and 1 quart warm water.

Expel Odors

◆ Kitchen odors disappear thanks to the freshening power of lemons and a few spices. Fill a small pot with water. Add several pieces of lemon rind and about 1 teaspoon each of McCormick Whole Cloves and Rosemary Leaves. Bring to a boil. The aroma will soon reach to nearly every room of your home.

- Freshen the air in your kitchen with the simplest of methods. Heat oven to 300°F and place a whole lemon on the center rack. With the door slightly ajar, let the lemon "cook" for about 15 minutes; turn off oven. Let lemon cool before removing it.

- After cleaning your wood cutting board, rub a bit of ReaLemon Lemon Juice on it to help get rid of garlic, onion, or fish smells.

- Add 4 teaspoons ReaLemon Lemon Juice to the water in your humidifier to eliminate stale odors.

PROJECT BATHROOM

- To remove soap scum from the bathtub and tiles, rub the surfaces with a cut lemon. To keep these areas free of soap scum, rinse them thoroughly after each use.

- The same method—rubbing with a cut lemon—can remove many sink and tub rust stains. For more stubborn rust stains, make a paste of ReaLemon Lemon Juice and 20 Mule Team Borax. Apply with an O-Cel-O No-Scratch Scrub Sponge; scrub, then rinse. Toilet stains can be removed with this same paste.

- To remove mineral and mildew stains from a shower curtain, first soak it in salt water for 15 to 20 minutes. Hang to drain excess water. Rub the stains with ReaLemon Lemon Juice while the curtain is still damp. Finish cleaning the curtain as usual, be it wiping with a damp O-Cel-O sponge, rinsing with clean water, or running through the washing machine.

Cooking and Laundry

Many a recipe calls for a citrus fruit or its juice. Some laundry detergents contain the cleaning power of lemon.

Welcome to the world of Way Beyond the Obvious! Citric acid keeps produce from turning brown and restores wilted lettuce. Lemon juice, tomato sauce, and milk work magic when you are concocting substitutions and facing cooking challenges. The whole gang of products can effectively tackle a sink full of dirty dishes, pots, and pans. Stains disappear when treated with lemon, lime, or milk.

Never fear. Domestic details are under control.

PREPARATIONS

◆ Cut fruit will stay fresh in the refrigerator without turning brown if you coat it with ReaLemon Lemon Juice.

◆ Here's another method to keep cut-up fruit and veggies from turning brown: Fill a bowl or container with enough water to cover the pared produce, then add 3 tablespoons ReaLemon or ReaLime juice.

◆ Freshen wilted lettuce by soaking it in a mixture of cold water and a few drops of ReaLemon Lemon Juice. Chill in refrigerator for 30 minutes.

◆ Put down that chisel! There's a better way to deal with a bag of hardened brown sugar. Simply put 1 or 2 apple wedges in the bag, then seal and store at room temperature. In a couple of days, the sugar should be softened.

◆ Keep potatoes from sprouting by storing apples with them.

◆ Return frozen fish to its original fresh taste. When thawing, cover it with a small amount of fresh milk or with a mixture of ¾ cup water and 1⅓ cups Carnation Instant Nonfat Dry Milk.

Tart Tips

◆ Before you stow uncut lemons in the refrigerator, put them in a jar of water. They will be juicier and will last longer than lemons stored in the produce drawer.

◆ If a lemon is too firm to juice, try either of these methods: Microwave it on high in 10-second increments until soft enough, or boil it for a few minutes.

◆ To get just a few drops of juice from a lemon or a lime, pierce the whole fruit with a toothpick. Squeeze out what you need, then use the toothpick to plug the hole. Refrigerate.

CREATIVE JUICES

Substitutions

◆ Whip up an easy sour cream substitute: Add a little ReaLemon Lemon Juice to a tub of Cool Whip. Let it sit for 30 minutes, then serve.

- Here's another substitute for sour cream: In a blender or food processor, combine 1 tablespoon ReaLemon Lemon Juice, 1 cup cottage cheese, and ⅓ cup buttermilk. Mix for 2 minutes.

Juicier

Hold an orange under hot water for a bit before you squeeze it. You'll get twice the juice!

- The recipe calls for buttermilk but there's none in the fridge? No need to change your plans. To make 1 cup buttermilk, put 2 tablespoons ReaLemon Lemon Juice in a glass measuring cup. Add enough low-fat milk (1 or 2 percent) to equal 1 cup. Let sit 15 minutes.

- Here's an easy way to make low-fat whipped cream: Beat 1 cup Carnation Instant Nonfat Dry Milk with 1 cup ice water for about 5 minutes. Serve immediately.

Tricks of the Trade

- Keep rice from becoming sticky by cooking it in water with 2 tablespoons ReaLemon Lemon Juice.

- If you add a small amount of ReaLemon Lemon Juice

Tears from the Joy of Cooking?

Kitchen supply stores sell goggles specifically manufactured for the purpose of shielding a chef's eyes from the tear-inducing fumes of onions, but some cooks use goggles made for welding or the chemistry lab.

Other tips to curb crying while peeling and cutting: Sharpen your knife, use only fresh onions, soak them in water or freeze them for 10 minutes beforehand, peel them under running water, light a candle nearby, or chew a piece of bread or gum while cutting.

to the cooking water, beets and red cabbage will retain their color.

- Before you cook chicken, rub a wedge of lemon over it. The result will be a juicier, more tender dish.

- Use up leftover cranberry sauce (say, after Thanksgiving) by making a meatball sauce from 1 cup cranberry sauce and 4 ounces Contadina Tomato Sauce. Heat and stir until fully blended.

- When boiling cauliflower, add about 1 tablespoon milk to the water. The veggie will stay white.

WASHING THE DISHES

- Soft cheese or other sticky food stuck on a grater? Cut a lemon in half and rub the pulp side on both surfaces of the grater.

- Reduce the chore of washing a greasy baking dish or pan. After the grease is drained off, rub the pan with a thick slice of lemon or a used lemon half turned inside out. Wash as usual.

- To clean the inside of a teapot, add the peel of 1 lemon per 2 cups warm water. Soak overnight.

- To remove rust from knives, cast-iron pots, and other kitchen equipment, make a paste with 1 part ReaLemon Lemon Juice and 2 parts Morton Salt. Apply with a clean, soft cloth and rub away the rust. Rinse with clear water; dry well.

- Protect aluminum cookware from being darkened by harsh cleansers. Wipe a clean pot with a cloth dampened with ReaLemon Lemon Juice; rinse well and dry.

- Remove the "rainbow" from stainless-steel pots by rubbing with a cut lime.

- To make stains vanish from aluminum or enamel cookware, fill the pot or pan with water and add a cut lime. Boil until the stains are gone. For a small pot, use half a lime; for a larger one, use both halves.

- When aluminum pans get dull, return them to their original brightness by boiling apple peelings in them.

Johnny Appleseed

Much myth surrounds the legend of Johnny Appleseed. The real-life John Chapman, on whom the legend is based, did collect apple seeds from Pennsylvania cider presses. He sold some, gave some away, and used the rest to start great apple orchards in the Midwest. Born in 1774 in Leominster, Massachusetts, as a child he met Samuel Wilson...the man who, decades later, became the real-life inspiration for Uncle Sam.

LAUNDRY DAY

- Adding 1 cup ReaLemon Lemon Juice to the washing machine along with the usual detergent may help reduce rust stains on your clothes.

- Conquer a rust stain with this pretreatment. First, boil water in a teakettle. Wet the stained area with ReaLemon Lemon Juice; hold it directly over the steam from the kettle. The steam can be quite hot, so be careful not to burn yourself.

- To remove a tough juice stain, mix ⅓ cup ReaLemon Lemon Juice or Heinz Distilled White Vinegar with ⅔ cup water. Soak the stain in this solution, then wash as usual.

- For tough stains—including mildew—make a paste of ReaLemon Lemon Juice and Morton Salt. Apply to the stain, set the item in the sun to dry, then wash as usual.

- Oil stain got you stumped? Dip a wedge of lime in Morton Salt and rub the spot. Launder as usual.

- Ink stains usually respond to a soaking in milk. Depending on the stain and the fabric, complete removal can take from 30 minutes to overnight.

CLOTHING CARE

- To put body back into your permanent-press clothes, dissolve Carnation Instant Nonfat Dry Milk in some water and add solution to the final rinse of your washing machine.

- Use ReaLemon Lemon Juice to clean and shine black or tan leather shoes. Apply with a soft cloth.

- Dip a clean, soft cloth into milk to clean patent leather shoes. Let dry, then use the cloth to buff the shoes to a shine.

House and Home

"Home life" is about much more than bricks and mortar (the physical properties that compose your apartment, condo, mobile home, or house), and lemon juice realizes that. In addition to lemon juice, there's a whole crop of products—fruits, veggies, milk, and peanut butter—you can turn to while maintaining and repairing your "homestead."

The lively side of home life also gets its due from these products. From crafts (drawing with lemon juice) to pet care (make a treat for your parakeet with peanut butter) to fitness (get your bike in shape with lemon juice), your kitchen is the star of the show.

HOMEOWNER HINTS

◆ When trying to sell your house, use aromatherapy to make your house more enticing to potential buyers. Shortly before a showing, put orange peel shavings in a pot of boiling water. Add a few McCormick Whole Cloves and Cinnamon Sticks, then simmer over low heat.

◆ Try this method to remove rust: Use ReaLemon Lemon Juice and Morton Salt to make a paste. Apply paste to rusted object and rub with a dry, soft cloth. Wipe clean.

◆ Before you throw out those old, hardened paintbrushes, try soaking them in hot ReaLemon Lemon Juice. As the bristles soften, comb through them with a wire brush or fork.

◆ Make the aroma of fresh paint vanish from a room. Chop a large, unpeeled onion into big chunks and toss them into a container of cold water. The onion *takes away* the paint odor—it doesn't replace it with its own bad smell!

◆ If part of a broken lightbulb is stuck in a socket, an easy fix is in your fruit basket. *First, make sure the electricity to the fixture is turned off.* Cut a small- to medium-size apple in half and push the cut side firmly into the broken bulb. Turn the apple and the bulb will unscrew along with it. Toss it all in the trash—don't try to remove the bulb from the apple.

◆ To clean a concrete sidewalk or patio, mix a solution of equal parts whole milk and Pepsi (not diet). Pour onto the surface and scrub with a stiff brush. Rinse off with a hose.

◆ A fine crack in a piece of china or a commemorative plate will eventually attract dirt and dust. First, make sure the piece is heat resistant. Place the plate or cup in a large pan filled with 1⅓ cups Carnation Instant Nonfat Dry Milk and 3¾ cups water (or enough fresh milk to cover the piece). Bring the mixture to a boil, then lower the heat. Let it simmer 45 minutes. The process? Cracks close when the milk reacts with kaolin, a soft white clay that's an essential component in manufacturing china and porcelain.

YOUR GREEN THUMB

◆ Plants watered with mineral-laden tap water or misted with fertilizer often have dull-looking leaves. Bring out the shine by wiping them with Dole Pineapple Juice or a citrus juice, using a soft cotton cloth.

- Nearly every plant benefits from an "apple shower." Mix 1 cup Mott's apple juice with 10 gallons water; spray on flowers, trees, shrubs, and lawns.

- Nourish flowering shrubs by burying apple peels and other past-its-prime fruit in the surrounding soil.

- To clean dusty houseplant leaves, add ¼ cup Carnation Instant Nonfat Dry Milk to 2 cups water. Dampen a soft cloth and wipe on.

- To keep your tomato plants disease-free, mix the following in a bucket: 3 cups compost, ½ cup Rite Aid Epsom salts, and 1 tablespoon ARM & HAMMER Baking Soda. Toss a handful into the hole when planting. Afterward, sprinkle some Carnation Instant Nonfat Dry Milk on top of the soil. Sprinkle on more dry milk about every other week.

- Spray outdoor ferns with a solution of 1 cup milk and 1 tablespoon Rite Aid Epsom salts in a 20-gallon hose-end sprayer. They'll enjoy the nourishing "meal."

CARING FOR YOUR FLEET

- To clean the chrome on your car, pour a small amount of ReaLime Lime Juice on a soft cotton cloth.

- Has cigarette smoke created a film on the inside windows of your vehicle? Clean it off with a solution of 2 tablespoons ReaLime Lime Juice and 1 quart water. Apply with an O-Cel-O sponge or clean cloth.

- Brighten unlacquered brass on boats with a paste of ARM & HAMMER Baking Soda and ReaLemon Lemon Juice. Rub on; let dry. Rinse well with warm water.

- Clean the rust from bike handlebars or tire rims with a paste of 6 tablespoons Morton Salt and 2 table-spoons ReaLemon Lemon Juice. Apply the paste to rusted areas with a dry cloth, then rub, rinse, and dry thoroughly.

PESTS INSIDE AND OUTSIDE

- To control an ant problem, squirt some ReaLemon Lemon Juice under the sink or in any area you see them coming and going.

- If you notice ants around a windowsill, paint a line across the sill with ReaLemon Lemon Juice. Ants won't want to cross that acidic line.

- When ants are taking over your lawn or garden, puree equal parts orange peel and water in a blender or food processor. Pour mixture onto anthills early in the morning.

- Hollowed-out orange and grapefruit halves can help you trap slugs and snails. Just before darkness falls, place them among your plants. In the morning, pick up the traps (with the slimy pests in them). Kill slugs and snails by dropping them into a bucket of soapy water. Toss the used rinds on the compost pile.

- An orange-based spray is an effective way to take care of soft-bodied garden pests such as aphids and cater-pillars. Put 1 cup chopped orange peel in a blender or food processor; add ¼ cup boiling water and liquefy. Let the mixture sit overnight at room temperature, then strain it through cheesecloth. Pour the liquid into a spray bottle, adding water to fill. Shake well and spray plants thoroughly.

◆ Protect your apple crop from maggots...with apples! Before the blossoms on your apple tree become fruit, buy some red apples with stems (2 for a dwarf tree, 6 to 8 for full-size). Spray them with an adhesive spray or coat with Karo Light Corn Syrup; hang them in your tree. When the adult flies land on the apples to lay eggs, they'll get stuck.

◆ Do you need mousetrap bait that's a little more enticing than cheese? Cover a Rite Aid cotton ball with Skippy Creamy Peanut Butter or bacon grease.

FRUIT OF THE IMAGINATION

◆ Have a child dip a Q-tips cotton swab in ReaLemon Lemon Juice and use it to write or draw on plain white paper. To make the design appear, hold the paper near a hot lightbulb. (Supervise children as they do this.)

◆ To keep bugs away when you're painting outdoors, add a few drops of ReaLime Lime Juice to the paint.

PETS ARE FAMILY TOO

◆ Make your own flea repellent by slicing up a couple of lemons and boiling them in 1 quart water. Allow to cool, run through a strainer, and put in a spray bottle. Spray on pets as needed.

- After cleaning up a pet accident on a rug or other area, spray it with a mixture of equal parts water and ReaLemon Lemon Juice to hide the odor and discourage repeat visits.

- Squirt undiluted ReaLemon Lemon Juice into your dog's mouth to discourage barking. Say "Quiet!" as you do this to emphasize your point.

- Most cats dislike the taste and scent of citrus fruits. Using this knowledge to deter kitty from biting or scratching will keep both of you out of harm's way! Prevent kitty from chewing electrical cords by first bundling them together and securing to a wall or floor to reduce the attraction; afterward, wipe undiluted ReaLemon Lemon Juice on them. If your cat is using its teeth or claws to "play" with you, spray yourself with a citrus body splash or a solution of lemon and water. Never spray directly at your cat.

- When Rover romps with skunks and comes home with the aroma to prove it, give him a bath in Campbell's Tomato Juice to kill the smell. Top it off with a rinse of equal parts Heinz Distilled White Vinegar and water.

- Make a healthful treat for your pet bird: In a blender or food processor, combine 2 tablespoons Skippy Creamy Peanut Butter, 1 cup mashed fruit, 2 tablespoons Sue Bee Honey, and 1 quart vanilla Dannon yogurt. Freeze mixture in ice cube trays (for small birds) or 3-ounce Dixie cups (for larger birds). At snack time, microwave 1 treat for a few seconds; place in cage.

Trademark Information

Argo Corn Starch® is a registered trademark of the ACH Food Companies, Inc.

ARM & HAMMER® is a registered trademark of Church & Dwight Co., Inc.

Campbell's® is a registered trademark of Campbell Soup Company.

Carnation® is a registered trademark of Société des Produits Nestlé S.A., Vevey, Switzerland.

Colavita Extra Virgin Olive Oil® is a registered trademark of Colavita S.P.A. Corporation.

Contadina Tomato Paste® is a registered trademark of Société des Produits Nestlé S.A., Vevey, Switzerland.

Cool Whip® is a registered trademark of Kraft Holdings, Inc.

Crisco® is a registered trademark of the J.M. Smucker Co.

Dannon® is a registered trademark of the Dannon Company.

Dawn® is a registered trademark of Procter & Gamble.

Dixie® is a registered trademark of Fort James Operating Company.

Dole Pineapple Juice® is a registered trademark of Dole Food Company, Inc.

Domino Sugar® is a registered trademark of Domino Foods, Inc.

GLAD® is a registered trademark of Union Carbide Corporation.

Hain Safflower Oil® is a registered trademark of Hain Pure Food Company.

Heinz® is a registered trademark of H. J. Heinz Company.

Karo® is a registered trademark of CPC International, Inc.

Kleenex® is a registered trademark of Kimberly-Clark Corporation.

Lipton Tea® is a registered trademark of the Unilever Group of Companies.

McCormick® is a registered trademark of McCormick & Company, Incorporated.

Morton® is a registered trademark of Morton International, Inc.

Mott's® is a registered trademark of Mott's Inc.

O-Cel-O® is a registered trademark of 3M.

Orville Redenbacher's® a registered trademark of ConAgra Foods.

Pepsi® is a registered trademark of PepsiCo, Inc.

Q-tips® is a registered trademark of Chesebrough-Pond's USA Co.

Quaker® is a registered trademark of the Quaker Oats Company.

ReaLemon® is a registered trademark of Borden.

ReaLime® is a registered trademark of Borden.

Rite Aid® is a registered trademark of the Rite Aid Corporation.

Scott Towels® is a registered trademark of Kimberly-Clark Worldwide, Inc.

Skippy Creamy Peanut Butter® is a registered trademark of the Unilever Group of Companies.

Sue Bee® is a registered trademark of Sioux Honey Association.

Tropicana Pure Premium® is a registered trademark of PepsiCo, Inc.

20 Mule Team Borax® is a registered trademark of The Dial Corporation.